A JOURNEY OF REMEMBRANCE

The Teachings of Ezekiel

As Shared With
J. L. Sibrian

Blue Feather Press
Edmonds, Washington 98020

A JOURNEY OF REMEMBRANCE

A Blue Feather Press Book

Printing History
Blue Feather Press edition: 1995

Library of Congress Cataloging in Publication Data
95-078299

ISBN 1-887592-02-4

Cover design by J. L. Sibrian
Graphic art by Vidya Gauci
Book design and production by Elaine Weston

To order additional copies of *A Journey of Remembrance*
Send $10.95 US dollars plus $4.00 shipping and handling to:
Blue Feather Press • P.O. Box 595, Edmonds, WA 98020 • (206) 781-5812

To be placed on the mailing list of the *Blue Feather Press* for future publications and seminars coming to your area, please drop us a note with your name, address and telephone number. Audiotapes of this publication will soon be available. For more information, please contact *Blue Feather Press*.

The author, J. L. Sibrian, may be contacted in care of *Blue Feather Press*.

PRINTED IN THE UNITED STATES OF AMERICA

CONTENTS

A JOURNEY OF REMEMBRANCE

INTRODUCTION

"Beloved woman. Be ye knowing of who you are..."
These words were spoken to me repeatedly on a cool summer's
eve in 1991 while I sat in meditation. I was relaxed and
focused and allowing, and so Ezekiel continued. *"These
words were spoken to you on this night, over and over again
as if in a mantra. For indeed, they are your mantra of
awakening, your mantra of becoming alive within God and
without God. You are it and all of it. This is not your ego, for
your ego would have you speak, 'I am nothing.' This is your
Christ spirit who speaks to you, who calls to you to be of the
knowing of who you are. Your journey is different than others,
though many share your eventual enlightenment by their own
path. We speak only to you on this night, only about you on this
night. Our love is focused on you. 'Be ye knowing of who you
are' is our prayer for you to awaken fully unto ownership of
God. For on this day of ownership, all else will open to you.
You wish to vision? We say unto you...feel! For that is your
true vision, the way you have manifested it to be. For only in
the feeling and the knowing of it will you become. This is your
path...your journey home."*

Through the eight years that Ezekiel has been with me his
messages have always been gentle, loving and honoring of
who I am. He has taken me with the utmost care through
feelings of unworthiness, doubt and fear. Ezekiel was first
introduced to me in a channeling class taught by my beloved
teacher Mafu, in August of 1986. From that time on we have

grown together. Ezekiel has been patient when I have been stubborn. He has been kind when I have been slow to catch on, and always, always, he has allowed me the space in which to become.

For years I had written messages from Ezekiel in notebooks and had tape recorded channeled sessions with a few friends. In 1993 my husband and I decided to buy a computer for Christmas. I sat in front of it one evening after work and opened myself to receive Ezekiel's messages using this medium and thus began the teachings recorded in this book.

It is my hope that those of you who read and share this book with others will grow in your love of God and love of self as God. The messages are simple. The truth always is. I encourage you to open your heart to the vibrational force of his words and be at peace with the knowledge that you are loved above all things. I am blessed to have been given the opportunity to share these messages with you. I wish you joy in the discovery of who you are in God's plan.

FORWARD

I have attempted in all cases to transcribe accurately the messages from Ezekiel just as they have been given to me. It is not his intention, so he assures me, to create a sexist book that does not address the equality of women in this modern age. The use of "mankind" and "man" throughout the teachings have been used to signify humanity as a whole and their frequency vibration as One. I know, from the time I have spent in Ezekiel's presence, that he loves and admires the feminine sex of which I am a joyful member. It is our wish that you will read these messages with an open heart and a renewed spirit and feel the love inherent in each word.

A JOURNEY OF REMEMBRANCE

ACKNOWLEDGEMENTS

I wish to take this opportunity to thank these special friends who have encouraged me along the way with their love and support. To Rosanne Lucero who was always there to lend an ear and gently guide me back to my path with her wit and wisdom, bless you my friend. To Carol Cumes who kept me grounded and humble and encouraged every step of the way. I treasure our friendship. To Dorine Owens and Roseann Ingraham who recognized Ezekiel's light from the beginning and were there to encourage his birth within me. To Betty Joseph and Mary Possley who helped me to laugh and to love his light once again when I would have forgotten to honor him. To my publisher and mentor, Janice Merrill, thank you for allowing me to become acquainted with a most exceptional woman and a new found friend. To Bud and Aaron for permitting me the space in which to feel supported and free to do this work. I love you both very much.

A very special thank you and profound acknowledgement to my most beloved teacher, Mafu, and to his blessed oracle, Ammagi. Without their love and commitment to the enlightenment of mankind, none of this would have been possible.

In dedication to you, Mom,

the brightest star in the heavens.

A JOURNEY OF REMEMBRANCE

A JOURNEY OF REMEMBRANCE

A JOURNEY OF REMEMBRANCE

THE ROBIN

Passing along the road one day, a young man beheld a fallen robin. The robin was not dead, just frightened and stunned from its fall to the ground. If you have ever truly watched birds, you know of the freedom and beauty that they possess when in flight. This robin was sorely imprisoned in its fall to earth. The young man approached the bird cautiously and with great reverence. He spoke softly and in a rhythmic chant as he began to ease the bird's suffering. Slowly and lovingly he picked it up. As he stroked its feathers, he began to speak of flying. He understood how wonderful the wind must feel when in flight, gently rustling the robin's feathers. He spoke of God's love for this robin and His wish that freedom and flight should always be his. As he spoke he began to blow gently upon the robin, reminding him of flight and freedom and all the things that were seemingly lost as he lay shivering upon the ground. With the breath of life surrounding him, the robin began to move. He stretched his wings and shook out his feathers and he remembered. 'I am this thing called flight, called freedom. I am this thing that God loves and I am nourished by His love.' With that, he lifted up into flight, never looking back. The young man continued to watch him go until he could see him no longer.

———————

You were always meant to fly, mankind, to love and to move in freedom and joy upon this plane. Let your Father's breath wash over you and bring this remembrance to life once more.

A JOURNEY OF REMEMBRANCE

A JOURNEY OF REMEMBRANCE

In the shadow of a great temple, there is always room for flowers to grow and life to continue. One does not always have to be in the great temple to proceed, though it is easier if they are. Some will need to listen to the chants and smell the incense from outside for awhile longer before they open up and walk inside. Their journey is not less than those inside, only different.

A JOURNEY OF REMEMBRANCE

I AM EZEKIEL

I come with the name Ezekiel for those who would remember this name from the Bible. For many, the Bible is the only connection they have to God. I wish that connection to be foremost in their mind when they speak my name. I come to teach them about God and their place in His heart.

I am Ezekiel and I come to bring you home, home to your Father who loves you....home to your rightful place in the universe. I come as your brother, your friend, your mirror. Do not turn from me mankind. Embrace me, for I am a messenger sent to tell you that you are loved above all things. I come to bring you closer to yourself as God. I do not come alone. There are many who are seeding the same garden.

We have wept for your pain, mankind. We have rejoiced in your triumphs. We come to teach you of other things. Who of you will listen and remember? Who of you will hear the call? Who of you will come with an open heart to receive Him who loves you? I am Ezekiel and I will tell you of many things. I will tell you of what I know, because I love you.

Here in the shadows of life comes a new beginning. We, of the Brotherhood, challenge you, of this earth plane, to rise above your station in life and reach for the stars. In so doing, you will reap the rewards that your Father has given you. These rewards are your birthright. Long, long ago when God first looked in upon Himself, He spoke, Why am I? You know the God of which I speak is you. In those beginning days, mankind, you were not yet formed. Only the thought of you existed. Only the thought of who I am, existed. I know what your journey has been, for I have done it.

Where am I now, this one who speaks to you thus? I am with you. I am the breath you breathe, the song your heart sings. Come closer to who I am within you and see the light that you are. Come closer. Do not be afraid. There are many, such as I, who wish to see you develop and grow into self-realization. That I come to you this way, through words on the written page and through the embodiment of this oracle, is my way of reaching inside you and planting many seeds. Some seeds will take hold and beautiful flowers will grow, memories awakened. Some seeds will lie fallow and wait for another Master to bring them to life. It is not my purpose to be your salvation, nor your Christ. It is my purpose to bring you home to the Father. It is my purpose to plant the seeds. Who will water your garden? You will, master. You will. No other can.

You have not come so far that you cannot still hear the words and remember. You are not so lost that your Father does not touch you in some way. You are part of your Father. Just as I am part of this oracle. She has allowed me to live more fully inside her for this purpose. There is someone calling you. Can you not hear it? Be in silence for a moment. Take the time to listen to His calling. Be at peace with who you are in all this. Know that your Father loves you as I love you.

Seek out another who shares your journey. Come together with others and create your shared energy and touch that place you thought hidden from you. Touch that place that only you will recognize as home. This is a joyful time upon this plane.

God is awakening and creating waves and waves of awareness among his people. These energy vortexes are coming together and will enable mankind to uplift itself into a new dimension of existence. You will know when it comes, for you will be as I am. You will know when it comes. Share your life with others who seek the light. Come together. That is your beginning.

Seek not your Father outside of you. Seek your Father within. He is your greatest seed. It is time now to bring Him alive within you. It is time now to sing your song with Him. It is time now to come home.

Sacred breath. Sacred sounds. Sacred times upon this plane. We have come here together for many purposes. We have come here to open up a line of communication from our Father to mankind. This will arrive through writings, through speech, through sounds and through participation in different locations and energy vortexes upon this plane called earth. Communication with the Father is accelerating at this time and is coming through in many ways, through many vehicles, through many men and women throughout this land. It is time now that mankind picks up the mantle of remembrance. The groundwork has been laid. The truths have been told. The vibrations have quickened. It is time now for mankind to put away doubts and to put away fear. It is time now for mankind to make a choice, to continue along the road that he has been making for himself into density more profound than any yet perpetrated upon this plane, or for him to make inroads into his Father's kingdom.

Some will choose density, and they will make this choice consciously, for unconsciously they have closed their minds to anything but what they see and what they feel. They do not pay attention to what they know to be true. So density is chosen and the road is long, and it is not a pleasant road. Some will choose to explore the possibility that there is more. They will begin to remember and begin to seek out those who will teach them that there is more; those who will teach them how to attain enlightenment and how to journey those journeys within that will become manifest without. We speak to those who will journey thus and we pray for those who have chosen another way.

I bring before you my oracle. She comes to you in simplicity and love. She comes with an open heart that has welcomed me inside for the work we do together. My purpose in coming is to bring her home to her Father. When first we began in the heavens, my oracle and I, we were as one in the beginning of all time. We separated to view who we were, reflected in each other's light. Forever, it seems, we journeyed thus, always together, never apart. Then in a blending of circumstances upon this earth plane, a cry was heard in the heavens. The people and the planet were dying. My oracle returned to earth. It was always our purpose to come together again in such a way that mankind would once again renew their connection with God in the vision of our light. Many share this same purpose.

My oracle is a bringer of higher energy. She is a facilitator for those in the presence of this energy, to go within and journey their journey thus, in the presence of God. She is a beacon. She is an open well so they can drink of this energy, of this lightness of being, and refresh themselves. She comes not, nor do I, to tell others how to live. She and I come together to tell the truth. That is all. She is a facilitator of spiritual growth. So we are here, my oracle and I. Come in our presence only with an open heart. Then you will know that we are all one with Our Father. So be it.

A JOURNEY OF REMEMBRANCE

A JOURNEY OF REMEMBRANCE

Behold thy light, for it shines brightly. Behold my partner in God. Behold God. I am with thee.

A JOURNEY OF REMEMBRANCE

MY PARTNER IN GOD

And so Ezekiel speaks to his oracle.......

Not so long ago you placed an order with me. You said that I was to contact you in this lifetime, at this moment of time, and that I was to make myself known to you as Ezekiel. You do not remember because it is almost impossible in this earth's density to remember anything! You spoke to me of your life and how you were going to serve mankind by becoming once again one of them. There was no dissuading you. You wanted me to watch over you and to keep track of what you were about, but not to interfere until you deemed it appropriate. I have kept my promise, although it has been difficult at times. Now you bid me come unto you. I am here. I did not know how difficult it would be to capture you once again and to bring you home. The fear is strong upon this plane. It is one of the strongest emotions known to man. This fear is generating more fear and manifesting disaster upon disaster. So here I am, attempting to bring one beautiful soul back to remembering who she is, and she is attempting to bring all of mankind home as well! Can it be done? Should it be done? Will it be done? So many masters have tried and some have succeeded to limited degrees. That they have tried at all is a wonderful thing indeed. Do you understand yet mankind, that you are worth it? Perhaps if you could vision more of who you really are in your Father's eyes, you would.

We are here, the Brotherhood, the Masters who love you, the humans who dedicate their lives to bringing you back to who you really are. We have always been here. You will come and listen and learn...or not. It is always your choice. Some of you fear that by listening to these teachings you are giving up something. You can never lose what you didn't have in the first place. It is all an illusion. It is all a mirage. You are in the desert seeking water and seeing only the illusion of the mirage in front of you. This plane of experience is not real. Oh, it feels real enough, for that is what you are here for, to feel. Emotions abound. There is only one truth and it is that your Father loves you and wants you to come home.

Where are we going? You and I are waging a war against forgetfulness. We are waging a war against sloth and resistance and sorrow. We are here to proclaim and to shout to the heavens. Mankind! Be ye knowing of who you are! Awaken unto the glory that you are. Manifesting God. Beloved entities. Born to experience upon this earth plane in such a way that your souls will never more return to density, for your Father would have you know all things. Your Father would have you saturate your journey of density and come home to Him, and begin to learn and grow in His light. Mankind, you are put on notice. Your life is going to change and change for the better! You will not give up anything. You will only gain and grow and love and laugh and become God! Is this not a wonderful thing?

Come here and stop for just awhile. Let me tell you a story. Mankind, you love stories and so I will tell you about who you really are. Once there lived a beautiful woman full of life and the joy of just being alive. She saw beauty in everything and in everyone. She was truly a happy human. Her family was not wealthy. Her circumstance was not stable nor filled with good fortune, still she was loving and joyful. There were not many around her who understood what she was about. Many would ridicule her and laugh behind her back. It did not matter, for she knew something that they could not even begin to remember. She knew God's love. She remembered God's love. She was God's love. It mattered not to her the clothes upon her back or the roof over her head or the laughing humans who could not see. She placed no blame on God for she understood that He was a most benevolent Lord who only granted peace.

So, mankind, do you think that this woman continued to live on the earth plane for very long? Indeed. She has continued to come back to this plane of existence over and over again in many states of being. Always she came as one who remembered God. Always she came in a capacity to awaken those who would continue to slumber. She asked little for herself for she knew that she possessed the greatest gifts already. Can you not remember such a person in your life? One person who you knew to be that kind of light? Think on it. If you can not see this person in your life, open a door so that she may enter and bring unto you a gift of life. She is waiting. You have paused long enough to read this. It only takes a moment to open the door to the possibility that you are really loved by God. Be still. Breathe deeply. Listen for the voice that will lead you home. Listen and hope and learn what she has to bring you. It is so simple mankind. So very simple.

You are loved by your Father. There is NO THING that matters more to Him than who you are.

Did you see yourself in this woman who loved God? Did you recognize that this is who you are in your purest form? Do not be afraid to contemplate your beauty. God sees you only as this light. He knows you only as this light. It is all that you are or ever have been. You have worn many cloaks over lifetimes. Never have you been disguised from God. You thought these cloaks were truly who you were. Remove those layers. Arise anew. You have only one cloak, the one your Father gave you. That is who you are. Light. Only light.

Mankind, make a promise to yourself. Promise to look for that place of remembrance. Promise to listen to that still, quiet voice within. Be in joy and happiness, for you are about your Father's work. Do not take another step in darkness. Your Father wants you to leave the light on. You have been in darkness for too long. It is alright to be brilliant and alive with love for who you are. It was always meant to be this way. Peace be with you and to the light that you are. I salute your journey home.

A JOURNEY OF REMEMBRANCE

A JOURNEY OF REMEMBRANCE

A JOURNEY OF REMEMBRANCE

There is a space in time which only love can fill, in which we become all that we have ever been and so we are cradled in this space and so we remember to remember. Be at peace. I am with you.

A JOURNEY OF REMEMBRANCE

SEEKING GOD

Be not afraid. Thy Lord is with thee. Walk with me beside the river of knowledge and drink from the liquid therein. Come closer to me and breathe in my song. I am within you. I sing the melody of you! The grass is soft and sweet to sit upon. You need not fear my presence with you here. Sit. Be with me for awhile. I only wish to sit beside you for a moment and drink in your essence. You are so sweet, mankind. You are so loved. Take some time to sit and be with me. I am here for you, to help you embrace the light that you are. You do not have to be so afraid that I will leave you again. You told me once, mankind, that you did not wish to know of what you could not see, of what you could not hear, of what did not fit within your life style. You told me to let you be, and so I did. But I have come once again upon you to love you and to ask you to sit with me and not be afraid. Are you still afraid, or are you ready to know who you are?

Some of you will stay in anger and fight the knowledge. Some of you, blessed souls, will listen and sit and remember and become that which you already are. Does it sound like I am making this up? No mankind. You know the truth of which I speak. You are my Father. You have come to this place in time to bring forth the adventure once again of seeking and finding God. How do we begin the search? First we sit in silence and open our hearts and allow our brethren from this side to speak to you. You will be surprised what an open heart will bring. Be not in fear when you hear the song of who you are, for it is truly a song born of many lifetimes of learning and loving and being. What a grand adventure you have all been on! What a journey! Sit. Be in silence. Open your heart and listen. Just listen. Then you will begin to know.

You have stolen my heart, mankind. You have come once again to experience fulfillment within the arms of God. You have come to Christ. You have done this before, many times. You are not yet ready to release this earthly experience, and so you repeat the coming and going of Christ upon this plane. So many lifetimes ago you began this journey. Some of you jumped ship, so to speak, along the way. Most of you stayed for the ride. To come and go, to Christ, to live and to experience emotions from your day-to-day existence here.

So here you are, once again getting ready to jump up and declare your existence as Christ. It is fun to play on this playground for awhile as man, but soon your souls begin to wonder what is missing. You are missing! Just as a child comes in from playing outside all day and sits to rest, so you have paused in your play to consider and to rest and to regroup. It is always wise to stop and consider what you are about. Look at the world as it is today, and you will know not many have taken the time to stop and to listen and yet their souls cry out. What does your soul cry out for? What say you that you are missing? Whose light do you follow? Whose song do you sing? There are many on this plane at this time who are ready to help you answer some of these questions. There are others who will take your money, feed you half-truths and send you on your way. Is this what you want? If it is, then embrace it and be in joy. Only then will you still retain a part of who you are and next time around you may glimpse more of the real truth.

What is the truth? Mankind, there is so much more to life than what you can see and feel with your senses. You have had some very big hints given to you lately in the news media, on talk shows, in books. Don't you get it? There is a major push afoot to wake you up, once again, and send you on your journey of discovery. Come closer to me while I whisper this truth. Mankind, you are loved and guided and cherished above all things. You are cradled in the arms of God. He wants you to know that you are loved and that you have played on this playground of limitation long enough. You are killing yourselves with drugs and guns and pollution. It is not necessary to do this to see your Father. You can come home to Him in wonder and joyfulness and peace. Is this not a wonderful revelation? Begin at the beginning with you and the Father. Sit with Him. Listen to Him. Breathe Him in.

There is so much to tell you. Where do I begin. Eons ago, when man was first brought upon this plane of dimension, he made a covenant with God that ever more would he seek to know himself as God. This covenant was agreed upon and so man began his adventure called life on the plane of demonstration. You are here now, existing because of this agreement, this covenant with God. Though this plane of demonstration called earth is not the only one that man has agreed to occupy, it is the one that you are focused on now, and so it is the most important in order for you to understand your promise. You live here as a guest of God. As a guest of God you are given everything. You are deprived of nothing. God is a grand host, a magnificent provider. He is welcoming you with open arms.

As a guest of God, the host, you are asked to do only one thing. What do you think that one thing is, mankind? What is the only thing that God asks of you in return for His hospitality? God wishes you to love, that is all. It is more than enough. Do you love, mankind? Do you care for yourself, and for your brother? Who is thy brother, mankind? Is he the homeless that you pass on the street? Is he the leper, the one with AIDS? Is your brother close to you in all things? Can you love who you are and share this love with another? These are difficult questions that I ask of you and you may not be able to answer them right now. You have forgotten much.

Come. Spend some time with me. Listen to what I have to tell you. As a guest of God, you promised to remember Him. You promised to see His reflection in all things. You promised to see Him in everything you gazed upon. Look into your mirrors and view the face of God. Look into the eyes of those you come upon and see your reflection there. God lives here because you live here, mankind. He lives here in every form. You are wise and wonderful and loved fully by your God. You were brave to come and be a guest of God. Though He is the perfect host, He expects you to remember who you are.

We have long gazed upon this earth plane with much inspiration and some disappointment. You have not always been so kind to one another. More so, you have not been kind to yourself. How can I make you understand how much you are loved by God? What can I do that will convince you to leap with joy for the revelation that you are loved and you are God and you are wonderful in every way?

Don't turn away, mankind, from the light that you are, the light that is being revealed unto you. Don't turn away. To do so will bring you great pain and grief. You have witnessed this in some beings already. Why would you turn away at all? The message is simple. The love pure. The motive, to bring you back to the full expression of who you are in reality. You are my Father. You came here to live out this wonderful journey called life! How could you forget who you truly are? You did not forget. You remembered just enough to seek out the truth when you were ready. God, as the perfect host, allows you to remember in your own time, in your own rhythm, in your own place. I am here to help you to remember and to follow your dream home to your Father.

In this age of enlightenment you are continuing to create for yourselves those activities that would seem to be counter-productive to your life upon this plane. All seeming disasters, be they flood, famine, earthquakes, fire or tornadoes, are all manifested from man's fear of ownership of his responsibility to life. Now you would say, and rightfully so from your prospective, how is this possible that we should bring such events down upon us? Mankind, if you lived totally in the awareness I and others seek for you, you would not. But we must work with what we have, and so we begin at the beginning. Step one: You, as God's most holy creation, manifest events in your life, both good and bad. Step two:

You, as God's most single-minded creation, tend to forget those things that you cannot understand. Though why this would seem to be so difficult for you to grasp is most interesting. Step three: You, as God's most stubborn creation, will not acquiesce to what you are shown if it does not fit into your most rigid set of rules. You continue to manifest disasters, death and drama, drama, drama. I could go on, but you get the point.

It is always most interesting to observe the thought processes that occur when a disaster is manifest. Mankind, in his collective consciousness, begins to gravitate toward an objective of sorts. We call this mind meld! This objective takes on form and density. It begins to coalesce into a form that will manifest disaster and the drama surrounding it. Reactions and emotions are recorded upon this collective consciousness and information is stored. Now you might say, because we have had so many disasters throughout the ages, don't you think we have stored enough information by now? Well, yes I do. The question really is do YOU think that enough information has been stored and registered in order to learn and to move on? Are you paying attention? The simplest answers are sometimes the hardest to grasp and the most unbelievable. Mankind, you have been told over and over that you are the creator of your own destiny, the author of your play called LIFE! It does not matter how many times you have heard it spoken. You are still playing out the mind meld of the collective consciousness that is performing acts upon this stage that may not always be the ones you desire. You may know the right way to think and to manifest, but you are only one in the consciousness of millions, billions of thought processes. Do not become concerned. There is yet a way around this.

Mankind, it is time to own your own thought systems. It is time to take ownership of your life and responsibility for your humanness upon this earth plane. You are much like children at times, lost in the act of creating and exploring and playing your game of life. You have forgotten much, that is for sure. Your Father is a patient Lord God. He is allowing and forgiving and loving. You have had your wings to fly and fly you have. There is nothing wrong with your journeys, they are beautiful to behold. What I want you to know, what I want you to remember, is that there is more. My beloved mankind, there is so much more! When I tell you that you are loved and honored in all things, what think you I mean? If it is your plan to continue along the path that you have set for yourself, that of exploring all possibilities, of melding with minds that are not yours, how can you begin to own your own destiny? You are one with the Father. Each one unique unto himself. You are dancing with others to a tune that is taking you farther and farther away from Him. I've come to tell you how to reconnect, if that is your choice, for your Father would not tell you how to play on your playground. Mankind! **Be ye knowing of who you are**. You are my Father, God's loving creation. He awaits you. He rejoices in your light, in your existence. He does not judge you in any way. He welcomes you to your home. Your home is within His loving embrace. It is time to turn your face once more toward His light, His love. Those of you who can do this will enable others to begin to remember and to return to the truer vision of who they are. The collective consciousness of mankind will begin to meld into a beauty and joy that you have forgotten to remember. This is a time for pausing and for re-evaluating your present existence. A time for reflection upon God. A time to renew your life.

How is it that you have traveled so far along this road called earthly existence and still you do not wonder more of the origin of this journey? Let me speak to this origin. You, as mankind incarnate, started from the love of your Master, God, to journey your existence on this plane and other planes as feeling, experiencing entities. This much you know already for there have been many teachers, past and present, who are here to teach and to remind you of this fact. So, here you are. Experiencing. Loving. Fearing. Exalting. Dying and returning yet again. You love this thing called experience! You love life so much that you return and return and return. The cycle repeats itself. The sun continues to herald a new day, the moon announces the night. You come again to live once more because it is familiar to you. It is much more familiar to you than where your origin, your path, first began.

I want you to begin to remember the origin of your birth. To do this you must first have a desire for more than this limited plane of experience can provide for you. You must have a desire to look past this emotional charge or that brief encounter with pleasure to a world that you have forgotten how to vision. Can you do this, mankind?

Your Father opens His heart to you. He opens His embrace so that you might come and view your origin without dying first. This light that draws you home does so to expand who you are, not to take anything away. You are so limited in your thinking, in your vision, in your curiosity. Our Father will not be truly happy until you come home to Him and begin to experience new and expansive journeys. To acknowledge that this possibility exists, is a beginning. Just as you are reading the words as they appear on this page, you are beginning to form an idea in your consciousness that begins to grow. The possibility that there is more. Oh, my beloved mankind! There is so much more!

Each step along the way brings you closer to the truth of who you are. That I say to you, "You are my Father," means nothing if there is not the self-discovery first. I emphasize the word *self* to illustrate your place in all this. Discovery does not come from inertia, it comes from movement. Self, or a sense of self, does not come from voicing the words of others. It comes from finding the words that are your own, embracing the thoughts that are your own, and from discovery and movement. Self-discovery is your ticket home.

How do I begin to grow? How do I begin the most important journey of this earthly existence? You have already begun, Father. If you put this book down now and never take it up again, you have already begun. The seed has been planted. The journey begun. Your Father has already placed a kiss upon your brow. He knows you and He sees you and He lives within you. You are His! Do not be wary of your Father.

He will not harm you, nor will He take away your free will. He loves you too much.

Stay with me a little longer and feel my joy and my reverence in your presence. You are God's most loving soul. You are God's brightest light. You are precious in His sight. He gives you life. Be at peace with the knowledge that you are loved.

A JOURNEY OF REMEMBRANCE

A JOURNEY OF REMEMBRANCE

A JOURNEY OF REMEMBRANCE

We come not as soldiers knocking down your door. We come as neighbors bearing gifts, gifts that you have forgotten to open.

A JOURNEY OF REMEMBRANCE

COMING HOME

I am Ezekiel who has come to stand along the platform and to gather up those entities who are ready to embrace the Christ within them and to come home. When I say to come home many may vision leaving this earth plane and returning to a heavenly existence and some may choose to do thus. Others may choose to walk as Christ here and in so doing touch many more lives and bring them home to the knowledge of who they are. They are God, heavily veiled to the connection of who they be as the Christ Spirit. This is a very different time than when our brother Jesus walked here. The energy upon this plane is not conducive to Christing or to coming home and it is not an easy time in which to live. These times may cause you discomfort of the embodiment and judgment from others as to how you live your life. You may be judged as being anti-social or not fitting into the mainstream, and happily you do not. You have chosen another way of being and you must always trust what you feel. You must stay within the confines and the boundaries of the energy that is allowing you to expand and grow.

This is a time of great difficulty upon the earth plane and many people are feeling the pull and the shift that is occurring and so you see on your news and read in your paper of heinous crimes being committed against mankind. The shift is being felt by many and some turn upon themselves and some upon others. That is the way in which they deal with the increase in energy. Others may at times become reflective and withdraw into a cocoon-like experience.

This planet called earth made a shift and the year 1994 showed a breaking away of many into community-like settings with people of like minds. You kept your individuality and your individual journeys, but you found a camaraderie among those who are experiencing the shift in a more positive spiritual manner than those who are dying in it. Many of the young people of today are being killed and transmuted unto another plane of existence because it is too difficult to stay during this time, so they are choosing to leave. You see the taking of life on such a grand scale and in such a heinous manner that it attempts to draw attention away from the other aspect of beingness, the turning toward God. The result is that man is becoming aware that it is too heavy a burden to carry, this turning away from God. Man goes to the church and goes to the meeting place and gathers together to light candles to remember a girl who was kidnapped and murdered, and this brings a community together. In reality, the girl has left this plane because she has served her divine purpose. There are many lights, such as she, existing around this planet. They are moving people to come together to experience camaraderie and love and to honor humankind. The man who took the life of this young girl serves the purpose of bringing these people together also. We call him wrong but they are both God at work and mankind must learn this lesson too. Mankind survives, humankind survives. Someone lights a candle and remembers. Someone gives a gift of life through their death, and mankind remembers.

This will be a day of new beginnings, of futures yet to come. December 31, 1993 heralded the opening of a window into super-consciousness. Though this window had been open for some time and began earlier in 1993, more awareness will now be placed upon this opening. We enabled mankind to proceed into 1994 with a renewed spirit, a renewed hope of his journey home. This journey home we speak of is not traveling to somewhere or leaving somewhere in order to begin anew. The coming home that we refer to is coming home to the knowledge of who you are. You are God. Though you hear these words and you speak these words, and you say these words in prayers, you have not yet come home to the idea; the knowingness of who you are. This is what this year will bring you closer to, coming home to that knowledge.

At this time there are many beings who are incarnating inside human entities who do not wish to continue in their embodiments. These incarnate beings are coming into already grown, adult bodies so that they may better prepare the way for mankind. This is happening universally throughout the world. These beings of light are incarnating inside functioning adult bodies whose only purpose was to come, prepare the body and the life, so that these beings could arrive at this time. This is a good thing and something that will enable the shift to occur globally. These seeds have been planted throughout the world in different locals, speaking different languages. These light beings are of a single purpose. They come to assist in the shift into super-consciousness and to maintain and hold the energy that is needed for the teachings and enlightenment to come forth at this time.

Sit for a moment. Close your eyes...Is it not wonderful that one can enjoy this silence and understand that in this silence one hears all things, knows all things, is all things. The silence becomes like a heartbeat. The rhythm of the heartbeat is broadcast and is touched by other hearts, and the synchronization begins so that the beat of many hearts becomes one beat, and the illusion of separation fades...and all that there is, is one heart beating. It is...enough.

Love one another. This is such a simple and uncomplicated message that mankind need never repeat it, if only he would gain the wisdom of simple things. So many lifetimes ago mankind was sent a messenger. This messenger spoke of the love that God had for His people, the love that God wished others to share. Do you not remember, mankind? You were there! God spoke through His Son to each of you. Love one another. Feed one another, clothe one another, shelter one another. Bind the wounds of thy neighbor. Look into the eyes of those you come across and seek the knowledge of universal love. You are so blind to those around you. I come to wake you up! You will hear of me and my oracle and of the teachers who have committed to bringing you home. We come not as soldiers knocking down your door. We come as neighbors bearing gifts, gifts that you have forgotten to open. Be prepared, mankind, I bid you joy in the discovery.

Jesus. Son of God. Jesus. Son of Man. They are one and the same entity. Here is your reflection, mankind. Here is the beauty and clear expression of your godhood. Speak not to me of who you think you are if you cannot first embrace who I know you to be. Jesus came as the full expression of the teachings of God to mankind. What did you learn?

First seek to know thyself as God. Enter the kingdom of heaven through this knowledge. Welcome home! Is it not a simple task that is laid before you? Seek. Find. Remember. God so loved mankind that He sent His "only" begotten Son, Jesus. Is this not how the story goes? Listen closely to something that is going to make you wonder about this story. Jesus was sent by you! He was your wake up call! Are you not brilliant? You sent Jesus to remind you of who you are. You are God. You made Him your icon. You worshiped Him. You loved Him. You feared Him. You killed Him. Why not? You sent Him!

Jesus...Jesus...Jesus...You became my mirror until I no longer wished to gaze upon You. Then I took You out! Mankind, you have continued to create Jesus for yourselves over and over and over. How has this been done, this creation of Jesus? You began to worship other icons that you saw as your reflection. Icons of great wealth, of great beauty. Each one has fallen by the wayside as you have gazed once again to find new icons to fill the void, to answer the question, *Who Am I?*

It is alright, mankind, to worship such things if they bring you joy. Joy is God. Listen. Where do you wish to be now? Are you happy with your life as it is? Are you in joy? Jesus lives! Have you not seen this written on the bumpers of your

cars? It's true, you know. He does live. If you created Him
and you sent Him to earth so many lifetimes ago, think you that
He will not come alive in the moment of recognition of
yourself as God? Of course Jesus lives. You live. It is enough
that you know this now as truth.

Mankind. You are bidden today to begin anew. You are
asked today to drop the mantle of forgetfulness. What is it you
have forgotten? You have forgotten who you are in your
Father's eyes. God loves and cherishes you beyond what you
have forgotten to remember. God is steadfast in His commitment to you. He has allowed you this journey into density, not
to punish you. He allows all things because He loves you and
wants you to know everything that He knows.

There are those who have not journeyed this density. They
have not gone far from their Father because in His sight they
had all that they required and all that they desired for themselves. These brothers and sisters, your brothers and sisters of
the light, took many forms. Some journeyed to find more
power. Some journeyed to find more joy. Some took on the
mantle of angels, helping mankind throughout the universes.
Some, such as you, journeyed density. Who does God revere
more? Whose path has been the truer?

Know you what God is, truly? God is who you are. God
is within and without. God is the light, the dark, the coming
of the day and the closing of the night. He is all of it. You are
all of it also. As many grains of sand as there are on this plane
are the journeys you are on. The trick is to journey, learn, grow
and move on. The funny thing about density is that it can

become a trap and has become so for many. If God loves us so, how can He allow us to become trapped? He does not. You have been sent messengers in every lifetime upon this plane. Some have listened. Some have not. While your Father would allow you all things, He would still step in to show you there is more. Always He prays that you will return to Him and to your knowledge of who you are in Him.

Once more the messengers come. This time they take on many cloaks, many guises. They do so in order to reach as many of you as they can. This is not an easy time upon this earth plane. Your density is great, your forgetfulness more profound than at any other time. Your Father wants you to come home to experience the joy and light that is your true calling. He will not choose for you. He will only provide you the opportunities to listen and to be exposed to the message He sends you:

Mankind. Walk with me again in remembrance of who you are. I love you and wish for you to come home now. You have journeyed long from me and from the joy and love that is your birthright. Come home and embrace who you are, as I embrace you. You are my joy, mankind. You are the expression of my love. Do not forget me. Do not forget the beauty that you are. Do not forget your Father who loves you. Listen to my voice. It is within you. Still yourselves long enough to hear my prayer for you. Come home to me. Come home to the full awakening of your power in love. Do not continue to give your power away to those who would abuse you. I have not abandoned you. You have forgotten to seek me out. Seek me out, mankind. Seek me out and be with me for eternity. See me in all things. See me in your countenance. I love you.

It is not a hard thing, mankind. Look around you and tell me that you have not forgotten your own power. Tell yourself in how many ways do you give your power away? How many pieces of yourself do you have scattered around? Gather yourself up unto the Lord thy God. He is where your power lies. With Him you are whole. With Him you truly begin to live. Live, mankind! Be in joy and thanksgiving and be in love! It is what brought you here. Do not forget. Seek out the messengers. They will tell you. Be a messenger! Then you will truly know!

A JOURNEY OF REMEMBRANCE

A JOURNEY OF REMEMBRANCE

A JOURNEY OF REMEMBRANCE

Dwell not in darkness. Seek the light and pull the darkness more into the light from your seeking.

A JOURNEY OF REMEMBRANCE

SELF-REALIZATION

Now is the time to begin anew. You are passing through a door. Enter the room and you will find what it is you seek. You cannot fail to see clearly when you move through this door. You fear that there is more of the same on the other side. More of the same density producing pain and a lack of peace. Hope is lost when you hesitate to move through the doors in your life as they are offered unto you. You cannot live for someone else. You cannot decide for someone else what doors they choose to enter. Choose only for yourself. Move through these portals in your own rhythm.

Suspend judgment of your place in life now. It is all a process that you are beginning to experience more fully. The energy around you offers protection for the light that you are. Do not fear what you cannot fully comprehend at this time. Your place is secured in the heavens. Your birthright is now expressing itself more fully in the energy exchange that is going on at this time on the earth plane.

Mankind is in a seeming state of suspension. They are moving neither backward nor forward. Mankind appears to have stalled, waiting to catch its breath for the next installment of experiences. This is not a negative thing, but a blessed resting space in which to gather strength for what is to come; and what is to come, you say? Oh mankind, you cannot even imagine the beauty and peace that awaits you.

Let me tell you a story about your life as it will be lived in this future time of beauty and peace. You will not know death as it is practiced today. You will come and go from this density in peace and with a renewed purpose to your lives. Many will seek to learn and grow in their alignment with God. Many will explore the heavens and discover new universes. The world as you know it now will not exist. This dream that you have held for so many years is coming to fruition.

How did this finally occur? How is it that you are to reap these rewards? How is it you have not had this blessed peace before? You have had this peace before mankind, but you remember it not. You have walked with God, but you remember Him not. You have been as God, but chose to forget.

A long time ago many of you pledged to come back to this plane and to pull the rest of mankind up from their depth of ignorance. You promised God. You are here to keep your promise. How will this happen? It will happen drop by drop, piece by piece, never stopping, always going forward. It is time now to reap the rewards of your life. It is time now to step up and declare who you are. Who are you, mankind? Indeed, I have told you that you are God. I have told you that you are creator and created. You have had great masters come here and hold you, love you and speak to you about this. It is the truth. The simple truth. The only truth. Everything else is just emotion. Everything else is separation. Everything else is false.

You come on this day to receive the wisdom of ages past and present. You come on this day to hear spoken the words that will bring you home to the truth of who you are. You listen. It is enough for now. The seed is planted within you. Your wake-up call has been sounded. You have called it forth. I am only the messenger. What greater love does god have for itself than to awaken from the dream and embrace the truth of who he is. It is enough now that you allow the space for this wisdom to take root and to begin to flower. It is enough. Your Father is pleased in the sight of you.

God has come to take you home. He has sent you many messengers from His kingdom to tell you that you are loved, to tell you not to forsake Him and not to forsake others. Your Father prepares a place for you. It is a beautiful place full of everything that you love. Come my friends, come and find your place with God.

You must realize now that this message I bring you does not mean that you will have to die before you can see your Father. Your Father does not wish for you to die at all. He brings you home through self-realization of who you are. He is gathering you up unto Him. He is gathering you up to realize that this is not death He seeks for you but life. Live! Live and love that you are!

Mankind, you thought that your lot in life was to live in misery, to live in fear and pain. It is not so and your Father wants you to know that there is so much more than you are now experiencing. Some may read this and speak, I am not in pain. Why should I seek to come home when I am happy here? Indeed, my friend, you should not. What your Father asks of you is simply to remember Him, for He knows that somewhere inside you is the seed of self-realization. This is what He speaks to, that kernel of self-knowledge, of alignment with Him. He seeks to water those seeds. Your Father grants you all things, even denial.

Why do I seem to speak the same truths over and over? Why do I spend so much time telling you of your Father's love for you? Why do I seek to tell you of self-realization? I come for no other purpose than to plant the seeds of your Father's love inside you. I will speak the same message to you in as many ways as I can. The truth is simple.

I come to speak through this oracle so that mankind can take advantage of a window of opportunity, an alignment of energies so strong as to enable mankind to better receive the blessings of their Father. The density upon this plane is thick indeed. It keeps many from seeking the light. It keeps many from realizing that the light exists. My beloved mankind, the light is there for you to see, for you to walk in, for you to become.

Do not worry so much about your life. Live it as you would, but live it in awareness of what I bring to you. Live it in awareness of what many masters on this plane are telling you. Take a moment out of your busy day and embrace the light that you are. Sit and be with your Father in love and in connection to Him. Speak to Him of what you wish. This is your time with Him. He is there for you. Ask your question and receive His answer. Say a prayer from your childhood, remembering a simpler time. Hold God in your heart. You are so loved, mankind. Take a moment to reach out to Him and lay your hand in His. Feel Him. Taste Him. He is your Father!

Many years from now when you have moved beyond the density of this plane you will look back upon it and wonder that you fought so hard to stay. Surrender to God. This is your mantra. It is now that God calls you to put aside this density and embrace another source. Embrace the light. Then you will know, then you will feel Him inside you. But first you must sit and seek Him in the silence. Come together with others who also search, or be in solitude. It matters not. What matters is that you take the time, make the choice, commit to another way of being.

I can only speak to you of what I know. It is your journey. It is your homecoming. I love you, mankind, that is what has brought me here. I love your courage, your strength, your outrageousness. There are no others in all the heavens that compare with you! I love that you are, and it pains me to see you in such density, such darkness. So, I have come. One messenger among many to light the candles of remembrance. I come to pass the torch as one once passed it to me. I come for this oracle who took on your form to bring you home in a way that you could vision and touch with your limited powers of perception. She has taught me much about how you think. That she and I are merged in such a way that brings insight to others is not something that has been done before in such a manner. This oracle and I are one in the kingdom of God. We are one here also, yet separate. We are the illustration of which I speak. We are mankind in its self-realization as God. This is the purpose for this book and why I come to you in this way. Self-realization of yourself as God is your journey, mankind.

It is time to stop for just one moment, breathe and become one with your Father.

Close your eyes for just a moment and feel God enter you as the Holy Spirit calls out for you to remember. Take a moment to recall what is so very important in your life right now, that you cannot speak God's name and be with Him in silence. He is here to come upon you in silence and unconditional love of who you are. Weep no more for Him. He is here with you now. He hears you when you call His name. He hears you when you forget that He is there. He knows you when you forget who you are. Your Father is in love with you. He waits gently and quietly for you to acknowledge Him for just a moment. He wants you to know that in that acknowledgement of Him, you realize who you are.

Who are you that your Father loves you so? Who must you be that He waits for you? Who, indeed. You are the most loved and cherished among His stars. He has scattered His seed amongst the universe and watched it grow into wondrous things. He wants you to know, mankind, that He has not abandoned you. Quite the contrary. He sends you many messengers with but one message. God loves you. That He wishes to express that love to you and wants you to acknowledge who you are is His gift, His prayer for mankind. Do not fail to take a moment of your time to welcome Him into your life.

Fortune smiles upon thee, mankind. Fortune comes in the form of many entities who have arrived upon this planet to assist you in the dawning of a new age upon this earth plane.

Fortune smiles upon you in the person of this oracle who is assisting the information to come full circle once again and to bring you back to the bosom of your Father. Seek not the false prophets who will speak to you of doom and gloom. Seek not the heritage of lifetimes that have brought you back here to repeat lessons and journeys which you must certainly have saturated by now. Mankind, none of you are new to this density. You have journeyed, all of you, many, many, many lives upon this plane, as well as others.

It is time now to allow fortune to smile upon you and to be done with limit. Limits that you have put upon yourself are not limits from God. You have continued to express yourself in the manner of human upon this plane in order to grow through emotion; to grow through feelings. Stop for a moment and ask yourself whether or not you are spinning your wheels. It's alright to love your life and to rejoice in it, but you would not be seekers of this wisdom we bring you if you were truly in joy with who you are right now. You have sought out this wisdom because you know that there is something missing. You're right, you know. There is something missing.

I have spoken to you before that you are my Father, journeyed in density, lost in feelings, circling over and over the karmic wheel. Who do you think designed this karmic wheel? You did! It is time to get off this treadmill and to rejoice in something else besides your accomplishments in density. Are you willing to take the chance that if you get off this treadmill of karma that you will live a richer life? Do you know, or can you even imagine what a vision we hold for you on our side? Do it now, mankind. Do it now.

So Ezekiel, you say, how do I get off this treadmill of karma? You make a choice and take the plunge. You sit with me in silence. You pray. You dream. You imagine. You become. Impossible you say! Oh, mankind! It is very possible and your window of opportunity is now. You are not abandoned by God. You must begin to reestablish a connection with Him. What is so important right now that you cannot put this down and sit in silence and joy with your Father? He is waiting for you. He knows your name. He seeks you out because He loves you. It matters not your life. It matters not, your judgments of self. All that matters is that you open your heart and let Him live once more inside you.

My beloved mankind, seek and you shall find peace, joy, love, happiness. It was ever thus that your Father created you in His image to experience all that you are....He is. Be in silence and remember a prayer you said as a child.

> *Now I lay me down to sleep.*
> (You have been asleep for a very long time.)
> *I pray the Lord my soul to keep.*
> (He has never left you, nor you Him.)
> *If I should die before I wake*
> (If you should pass from this earth once again before
>   you wake up to who you are.)
> *I pray the Lord my soul to take.* *
> (Your Father will rescue you.)

Mankind, this is the prayer of a child in all innocence and

---

* Traditional prayer, author unknown

connection to the light. This is also your prayer of reconnection.

Be in peace with what I bring to you. Be in joy for your awakening. Prepare thyself to experience joy as you have forgotten exists. Sit. Be in silence. Listen, mankind, your Father calls you to come home not in darkness and not in death, but in life! In your search for God you have a right to know that He is filling you up. Much as a vessel is filled with the purest of water, so you are filled with the purest of light energy, the loving source of God. Find a quiet space for yourself. Begin to breathe slowly, rhythmically, in and out. Taste the breath upon your tongue. Savor it. Feel how your body responds to this breath. Listen for it. Feel it. Close your eyes. Breathe deeply. Relax. You are safe. All is well. Breathe in your God. Fill your cells with His light. See these cells in your mind's eye, how they grow in His light. Breathe in and out. Be in love with your Father. Feel Him! Listen for Him. He is here. Do not speak. Do not move. He is within you. He is surrounding you. You are His. He comes in love to embrace you. He comes for you. Be in love with who you are. Experience it all. Savor the moment. It is beginning. So be it.

Many lifetimes ago you journeyed the journey of God. You have forgotten much, that is for sure, but not so much that you could not call for Him and He would be there. You are in a dream, mankind. You are in an incredible dream of separation. There is no separation. I will wake you gently from your sleeping state until you are in full realization of the power you possess.

Be patient and steadfast. There will be no trumpets to herald your arrival, only a silent song sung by the breath moving in... and out... and in... and out... reminding you that your connection to the Father has never been broken. You are His and He is yours. Is this not a wonderful thing? Sit with this awhile before you go on. Take time to be. In this state of beingness, you will know. You will remember how it feels to be whole again. It is ever so that god speaks in every lifetime: "Why am I here? Where have I come from? Who am I, really?" And it is ever so that messengers are sent to teach these truths and to answer those questions posed by god, in the body of man and woman. You have all walked this land for lifetimes. You have walked other lands in ancient and future travels. How do I speak to you when you know so little of who you are, and when you are experiencing not but a small portion of yourself in reality? How do I bridge the large chasm that divides you from what you know now in this density and what you truly are?

Man and woman were placed here by benevolent gods, by loving and joyful spirits. Man and woman were placed here by you to journey, experience and to feel. This was the grand plan. You were never to forget so much! Mankind in all its glory on this plane is nothing when compared, if you would compare, to mankind in the kingdom of God. Would you not like to vision this glory? Would you like to know how to tap into the truth of who you are? Venture thus with me for awhile, and I will teach you many things about yourself.

When first you came upon this plane of existence you were

connected wholly to God and to the God Force. Your light stretched out into the heavens and beyond. It was glorious to watch you at play in this experience called density. You were not so unaware then, not as much as you are now. For thousands and thousands of years you played and learned and experienced. You journeyed back and forth between conscious and unconscious behavior. You were never so unconscious that you could not still remember, but you played with that also. You enjoyed your games and your intrigues, and all in the heavens and beyond learned and grew from your experiences. What joyful creatures you were!

Over time, some of you became bored and decided to play another game. This game was called control. You began, some of you, to vision a different journey for mankind. You wanted to rule over the destiny of others. You became filled with your own desires and your own set of rules. It was a new and powerful feeling and one you continued to enjoy. There were still those innocent souls who were traveling back and forth from the heavens to the density and enjoying the ride immensely. You, those who wished to control, tended to stay more in the density and to plan the traps for the innocent ones. Your numbers began to grow and soon you were in control. Some escaped and returned to the Father; many did not.

So here you are, reading this book and wondering how you got to such a place in time. Were you the controller or the controlled? Well, let me tell you. You were both, for this is a land of experience and emotion. You were here to experience equally, so there is no pointing of fingers or feeling of superiority. You controlled and you were controlled, much as in this lifetime you have experienced both emotions.

So where does that leave you now? Who are you at this time? You are my Beloved Father waking up! Mankind, in order to move beyond density, you must fully realize how brilliantly you have evolved to this place in time. You must realize this without judgment or regret. This is part of what holds you back from fully regaining your divinity. How can anything that has brought you experience be judged when it is the full purpose of your existence here? Stop judging and learn what it is you need to learn and move on. There is no one in all the heavens who judges as harshly as you. You were never intended to stay so long in this place anyway.

Mankind, you are loved and watched over by many. Some are with you on this plane to bring you home to the wisdom of who you truly are, by enabling you to see with a vision that you have forgotten how to use. This vision is your inner vision, your inner teacher, the brilliant god that is seeking to know more than it yet realizes. Some of these messengers will register in your knowing heart and you will see. The truest messengers will not tell you how to think, nor will they tell you to follow. The truest messengers come only to ignite the flame that burns inside you. You are your deliverer. Would you have me tell you the recipe for enlightenment or would you like to explore the possible combinations for yourself? This is what I wish for you, that in the exploration you will see the light that I see when I gaze upon you.

I love you greatly, mankind. You are here this time for a

purpose that is more profound than any you can remember. You are here to realize who you are in your Father's life. This is a grand and noble adventure. Seek to know you as I know you and you will find the love that I see, the light that I know, the god that I need to be complete.

When first we began, my oracle and I, to journey thus for the enlightenment of mankind, we were naive to think that it would be easy. It is not easy, and so we have chipped away at the layers of debris that have filtered through and settled on mankind. This is a quest for cleansing as well as enlightenment, for one cannot occur without the other. So we chip away and know that underneath this mantle of forgetfulness is God unaware.

It is enough for now just to know that we are here, many of us, chipping away, layer by layer. Mankind, you must be worth it or why else would we spend so much time and energy? There are many from my side who would say, why waste your time? Let them evolve or devolve until they decide to return to God. It is not altogether an unappealing stand at times! But, mankind, you have great champions on this earth plane who bring Masters such as I to do your bidding, in the hope that you will realize who you are and come home to know yourself as God.

What holds you back from this realization? Do you believe that Jesus was here only to die for your sins? No, mankind. He was here to wake you up and to show you who you are in His sight...you are God. This is not so difficult to grasp when you look at the life of Jesus. He was all things. He was mankind

in its self-realized form as God. You idolized Him. You
cursed Him. You ignored Him and His message. You held
Him above you when in His life on this plane He walked with
the simplest of you...the lepers, the disenfranchised, the homeless. Jesus did this to show you...what? That you were less
than He? That you could never be who He was? Jesus loved.
That is all. He loved His Father. He loved who He was in the
sight of His Father. He loved mankind, who He knew to be His
Father. That is all. He loved....He loved.....He loved.

There are some stories of Jesus that were not written in your
great book. These are the stories that mankind would never
know. These stories told of the mystical and magical side of
His life. They showed those who followed Him a new way of
being with the Father. He studied meditation and communion
with God in all forms. He spoke of reincarnation and karma
and moving through the wheel of life. These are the stories
that you will not read in your great book, but these are the
things that He was about also. It is alright and has not been said
to anger some who would feel lost in the knowledge that not
everything was written down of His life. It is said to plant a
seed and to open a door of possibility, so that growth may
occur. That is the only reason.

Mankind, you are much on your Father's mind. You are
much in His heart and He attempts to breathe life into you. He
sends you many messengers. He always has. Pay attention to
them as they may come in the guise of a child, an animal or
even a sunset! The simple truth is that your Father is every-
where within you and without. Be at peace with this knowl-

edge and seek Him out often. Yes, there are many dark and
seemingly evil things that are occurring also and have always
occurred throughout time. Our Father would speak that in all
light there is darkness and in all darkness there is light. This
is an ancient understanding. Dwell not in the darkness, seek
the light and pull the darkness more into the light from your
seeking. That is how it is done. First you acknowledge, then
you act. In the action God is born. It is enough now for you
to know.

A JOURNEY OF REMEMBRANCE

A JOURNEY OF REMEMBRANCE

Speak not at twilight that you have not known God this day. Speak only truth. That as you have lived on this day, so has God lived. There is no difference.

A JOURNEY OF REMEMBRANCE

REMEMBER THE LOVE

Night comes as soon as it is bidden by the moon's ascension to the wandering sky. You feel the night descend upon you in a moment of silence, as darkness covers you over with its blanket of stars. You are appeased, all is right with the world. Man is satisfied that he is once again within the parameters that he has set for himself. As the sun rises, day appears. As darkness falls, it is night. Many ancient peoples feel that day and night are brought by gods, and so they are correct. They worship these gods as if they were separate from them and somehow less than they are. It has always seemed to serve man to think thus and so he has, secure in the knowledge that he is at the mercy of something greater than he.

God is great. Of that there is no doubt. He has created you in His image out of love for who He is. Can you not feel this love and hold it in your heart long enough to consider the possibility that you are worthy of creating your own day and night, your own destiny? God does not want you to worry so about the coming and going of the day. He is present in this day and wishes you to be present in it also. What does it mean to be present in the day? God notices everything. He forgets nothing. All things are of equal importance to Him. When you experience His presence in the moment, He is alive within you. Make way for God!

Shadows appear and you forget to notice the flower, a child's laughter, the rushing brook. Erase your memory for a moment. It can be done. Sit with me in silence and listen, really listen. You are not alone. Caress this day. Explore your senses...be in silence. Do not forget to come close to God in this silent place. Open your heart, expand your ego mind to consider His existence within you. You are so loved and cherished by God. How could it be any different? Did He not send His Son to nourish you with His love? Yes, He died by your hand, for that is what man does. He kills because he fears. He fears because he wants to become comfortable with the day and the night in their rightful order. He does not want day to become beautiful and last forever! No, that is too frightening to contemplate. Mankind, you do not have to be so frightened. We will begin to teach you what you need to know to embrace that part of you that you are too frightened to look upon. We love you. It is a simple thing that we do, this teaching, but it will set you free to love and to be. Embrace who you are in this. So be it.

You are not alone. Have you not heard this phrase before? You are not alone. What does this mean? You are part of a much grander whole than even you can imagine. What drives mankind to seek this whole? What drives mankind is the emptiness he feels whenever he pauses long enough to ask, am I happy? You are not alone. Does this bring you comfort? No. I think it does not, for there is seldom much comfort in words alone. That is why, as these teachings take place, you will find yourself amongst like souls and a master teacher who will elevate your energy so that the words will carry much more importance. You will literally feel uplifted. "You are not alone" will carry a vibration that will register within your soul

and fill your embodiment with the knowledge of this whole-
ness of which we speak. It is not so much the words as it is the
tonal quality inherent within them. So you wait for that time
when these teachers arrive. I am giving somewhat of an
introduction to this "coming," so to speak. There will be many
questions and many answers to come. One of the teachings
will address the whole of which you are a part.

Mankind, you have waited a long time for this second
coming, this ascension of the Christ consciousness to arise
within you. You can be patient yet a while longer as we
prepare these teachers to spread the word. This is an exciting
time upon the earth. A new beginning. Actually, an old
beginning that is being reawakened. You have the knowledge
of the very first breath within each of your cells, the first
sound, the first instant of emotion. It's all there waiting. When
you reach back into that place of beginning you will yet
embrace more than you realized you had ever known. Mankind, be happy! This is a wonderful thing that is arriving on
this planet. You have some wonderful teachers who have
prepared the way and some that are yet to make their presence
known. We watch you, mankind. We pray for you. We love
you and we want you to remember that you are part of this
whole. You will soon know and then you will not be afraid to
love who you are. All that you will see will bring you joy. Is
this not a grand adventure yet to come? You have become too
complacent and too reluctant to hope. Hope is a very important thing. Without it you will never reach out to touch that
which you are. You are God. You are not alone. We have

come to gather you up unto your Father. Then you will know. Then you will see. Then you will remember.

There is a little known truth that needs to be shared at this time. In this third dimensional existence you are cognizant of what you feel, know, sense and experience within the realm of your limited understanding. You are limited, because to be otherwise would make it impossible to exist on this level. Come now, and journey thus with me as we step toward the possibility of the dimension that exists parallel to this one, but vibrating at a more accelerated knowledge of awareness. On this level of awareness you are able to see more clearly thy brother and what he is about. You speak not with words so much, as with thought projections. This enables man to live mostly in truth. I say "mostly in truth" because it is very difficult to deceive when others read your thoughts. On this level of existence man still tries to deceive, however. He does not see clearly, as yet, who he really is. There is still the fear and the questions and the yearning to know. Still it is a lovely place, not unlike this one you are on now. Your powers there are different, more enlightened. As you begin to expand your knowledge of what is and is not true, you change your perspective of the visions around you. You begin to grow and become more light within and without. It is a very peaceful existence. There is still more. Each realm, each dimension, affords you the opportunity to grow, to become, to explore, to learn, to move on. You are not limited to any of this now, even while you exist on the plane of demonstration called earth.

How is it that you may become more attuned to these other

realms? How do you keep from fearing that which you cannot or will not perceive with your earthly senses? Mankind, if you learn nothing else in this lifetime let it be this...God loves you. He wishes you no harm. He is there for you. You are His. This life you are leading is an adventure of spirit, an adventure of the soul. You have not changed in your Father's eyes. He loves. That is all He does. He loves. He judges not who you are or what you have done. He loves you. You are a part of Him, just as your arm is a part of your body. Could you judge your arm as bad or less than the whole of your body? God does not judge you because He doesn't know how. All He can do is love, and He loves you. When you reach the realm of higher consciousness, the realm from where God first birthed you, you will know that all that exists for all time is love. There is nothing else. The realms that you have passed through to finally come home can only give you the experience and teach you what they know and vision. That is why you must continue to search and to reach and to journey, until you come upon the place wherein your Father lives. If I spoke to you that this place was within you, you would not understand and so I speak of a realm, a plane of existence.

When first your Father birthed you, He planted a seed of remembrance called the soul within you. What was this seed to grow? Love of self as God. That is all. You took the seed and planted many other things. You planted fear, hate, jealousy, avarice, and with it came pain. You had forgotten the love of your Father, but He had not forgotten you. He remembers you still. In your journey back to Him, remember the love. When you are in fear....remember the love. When you hate, remember your Father and His love for you. Do not waste another painful moment doubting your Father's love. You can journey many realms of existence by living your life in this remembrance.

And so...what happens when you die? Where does your soul go when it leaves the body? Why, mankind, your soul returns to your Father! How is this possible, when it has been taught by so-called enlightened masters here, that we go to the level of understanding or mastery achieved on this plane and live out other adventures? Will we not sleep and wait for our Father to wake us up? Some will, for it is their belief. Will we not see Jesus and sit on the right hand of God? Some will, for it is their belief. You will return to the Father that loves you. That is the only truth. You will return to the absolute love of self as God. The seed that He planted brings you home because that is the only truth that there is. Your vision has become so clouded with dogma and drama and experience that you are blind to the simple truth. Ask yourself one question only, do you love God? Can you remember His love? In that instant of remembrance, you are home with Him.

All things that are not of love do not exist in God's kingdom. All realms of understanding that come to you from this vision are moved through quickly and without effect. These are the realms of fear and doubt. Do not doubt that you are loved, mankind. How could it be any different? Speak to God from where you are now. Do not wait for another time or another place to bring you closer to Him. He is here now. Call

Him and hear the answer in your soul.

It is ever so that mankind reaps what he sows. The harvest has been lacking of late in many of the aspects of God that are needed to sustain life. You are the one who plants the seed, who tills the soil, who reaps the harvest. How is it that you have lost touch with the only thing that can truly sustain life, love of God and love of self as God? This, of course, is only a metaphor for your life here in this density. It was spoken thus, so that you could form the image in your mind of the integral part you play in this evolvement back to the Father. When we speak, "back to the Father," you must realize that you have truly never left Him. That is an illusion. That you have forgotten to remember Him is the truth.

You have come forth on this day to remember. It is so, or you would not be reading this book. Let me explain something to you now. You are reached in many ways by the Father. I have spoken of messengers that He has sent in every lifetime. These messengers reach you in various ways, through various mediums. What is transposed into words or visuals, song or dance, is the vibrational force of God. All is energy vibration. That is how you are reached, that is how we proceed to involve you once more with us. Your job is to stay open and to be that receptacle. Do this with the highest intention, and only they of the light will reach you.

Let God play you as He would a most beloved instrument. Let His vibrational force reach inside you. Let Him strike the cords so that you may know Him truly. It is all vibrational frequency. When first you were birthed from the Father, you were as a note struck on a cosmic instrument. Your vibration sang with its own unique sound. You were born thus and there is no other like you in all the galaxies. Is it not wonderful that there are so many separate souls moving within this awareness of God, who weave a tapestry of such beauty that it can only be visioned with love? You speak with one sound, yet vibrate in your own uniqueness. Come closer to me, mankind, and to your understanding of purpose. Seek these messengers and allow them to ignite your spark, then move and become aware. Shed your cloak of darkness. This is the time and you are the voyagers.

There was a time, in the beginning of time, when all lands that were inhabited were connected to one another. The way in which they were connected was integral to their survival. They were connected to the One Mind, and in that connection they were able to flourish, never doubting who they were or what their purpose was. The One Mind of which I speak is the mind of God. God so loved the world and the people in it that He granted them the freedom to break from the One Mind. In so doing, man began to wander across the surface of the world. He began to explore new experiences and have other adventures. Soon he forgot the One Mind and his connection to all things, for mankind was too busy exploring. In the process, some broke free. They ventured thus, throughout the world, and came back with tales of great exploits. The others looked upon their brothers and saw that they were much changed, and they knew not these experiences and they became curious. God loves all of mankind as He loves all things of which He is a part. One by one He watched them go.

Have you traveled far, mankind? Have you forgotten so completely who your Father is? Are you so emersed in the adventure called LIFE that you will never come home? I am Ezekiel and I come to remind you of where you began. It was a far simpler time and a time of great beauty. This you do not remember and so it holds little appeal to you because you have forgotten much. I wish you to remember and to reach for that time and that connection with the One Mind and with your fellow man again. You are not connected, one to the other. Not as you were in the beginning. There is much violence and hate and so much sorrow. I weep for you because it does not have to be this way. Your Father has allowed it because He loves you. He has sent many with this message in an attempt to have you remember from whence you came. I say this to you now because there is a window of opportunity that has opened; it is being held open by the Lords in the hope that you will listen, and you will step forward and have the courage and the desire to remember your connection to all things.

Beloved Father,* all that I Am, you are. I am only here to show you who you are in this world that you have created. In the creation of this world you have manifested many things. Some of them have brought you peace and increased your joy. Some of these manifestations have brought other things that have not been in your best interest. Speak the truth to yourself when you gaze upon what you have created in your life. Do you have sorrow? Is your life joyful? Do you love? Are you loved? What is your life that others might know you from how

* Here Ezekiel refers to mankind as "Father."

you live? Speak not to me falsely, for the lie only keeps you from gaining knowledge of your right to beauty and joy.

Why do I speak to you thus? Why do I challenge you to look more deeply into this life you have manifested? My Beloved Father, I speak to you in this way so that we may gain knowledge of one another and, in this way, become whole. I miss you. I love you. There are many who gaze upon you and ask why. They cannot know unless you tell them. In this way we all grow. Learning does not stop here on this plane of density. It continues on many levels. There is often resistance found on these levels also. I challenge you to look more deeply at your life, not to criticize, but to grow in the knowledge of who you are. You are My Father, manifested upon this plane of density to come home. You were only supposed to play here, it was never meant for you to forget so much of what you are.

We are upon a crossroads, you and I. We are all interrelated, one to the other. As you grow and expand your consciousness, so the consciousness of all beings is enhanced. If you could look more closely at the interweaving of this universe, you would see how important each one is to the other. It is much like parents with a child; they pass on knowledge of what they have learned so their child can grow in becoming man/woman. It is ever so that knowledge is passed on.

This is why I come. This is why many come at this time. You are so innocent, mankind. You are so trusting that each day will arrive just as the one before. What if today was the

only day that was left? What would you accomplish then?
Would you seek to know more? I am not here to tell you the
world is ending. You have enough people who fill your head
with this truth. For it is a truth if you believe it to be. That is
how powerful you are, mankind. You can manifest what you
know, or think you know, to be true. If this were your last day
here, what would you wish to manifest for yourself and for
those that you love?

It is not a difficult thing that I ask of you, to be sure. The
difficulty lies in your acceptance of the responsibility of
change, of knowledge gained and acted upon. You are my
student, mankind, and you are ever my teacher. I marvel at
what you have perfected for yourselves here in this density.
You are remarkable for the ingenuity of your mind. I ask only
that you put this to work for you in another way. I ask of you
that you seek the truth of your life. Look at every aspect. Look
closely at the people in your life. Feel what they mean to you.
Vision what you see when you gaze upon them. Remember
that you are all interwoven, much as the fabric of the cloth you
wear. You are all a part of each other.

This that I ask of you, this challenge I give you, will open
many doors and lead you home if you will allow it. I do not
speak at length of these things, for I wish you to do the
thinking. I am only here to present the challenge. When you
find the answers for yourself, you will become empowered
and then you will learn all that you need to know. Your
strength comes in this empowerment. Seek not one who
would tell you that this is the way to be or to think. Seek only

the challenge and do your own thinking. I love you and wish for you a journey of joy and remembrance. I have come for this oracle. It is our journey together. She would have me teach what I know so that others might know it and seek their own truth. The only truth is what you know. You are God. I will stay as long as it takes. That is my promise to my oracle. I have much love for you mankind. You are worth it.

A JOURNEY OF REMEMBRANCE

A JOURNEY OF REMEMBRANCE

The dreamer is awakening from the dream...

A JOURNEY OF REMEMBRANCE

THE DREAMER AWAKENS

There is nothing that pleases me more than to view an open heart. To view a heart that is ready and willing to receive higher wisdom is a beautiful thing to behold. We are humbled by mankind in the awakening of all that he is. We see mankind for what he has always been, a divine presence, an aspect of God. We say an aspect of God because it is in your awakening that you begin to realize that what is projected here for you, in this lifetime, is but a fragment of all that you are.

In your surrender to God, in your receivership of His love, you are re-born or re-birthed into your own divinity. It is not an impossible thing to accomplish if you are willing to learn. These teachings that you surrender to will lead you to re-examine your life in such a way as to embrace a much broader view of who you are in the scheme of things...the cosmic scheme of things. Behold, you are more than what you now perceive yourself to be. May I be allowed to tell you what that is?

I speak to you as one who has seen and heard you call out to your Father for understanding, for love, for help. I have heard your prayers and watched you pray them. I have felt your pain and sadness and you have also allowed me to experience your joy. Beloved mankind, how can I reach you? What can I say that will allow us to continue to grow together in the understanding of what you are? I pray for you, mankind and I wait...we all wait. You are building a new road. You are building a new road into enlightenment. You go about picking each stone to lay upon your path so that your next step will be cushioned and secure. You pick carefully, with much fear. The fear that you feel is the fear of the unknown. What will be down this road, you ask? How do I know that I will not fail? Who is waiting for me if I complete my journey? Where does this road lead anyway? It is your road....you tell me where it will lead.

In the beginning of our journey on this plane my oracle and I made a plan. She would come here to the plane of demonstration and I would reside in the consciousness from whence we all come. We had lived long together in this Christ Consciousness and had forgotten how powerful the emotion of "fear" could be. Fear has been the single most powerful roadblock to mankind's return to God. In some instances, fear has been used as a weapon to keep man/woman from knowing and realizing their own divinity. It has been fostered and fed and used to control. No wonder that you are reluctant to believe what is so simple...you are God, the grand manifester of your own destiny, and the only one who can bring you home. Fear is your only enemy.

To relinquish fear, one has to open to the possibility that there is more than what he can see, hear, smell, taste and touch. You want your boundaries defined for you by someone or something that you have always believed in, or that you could perceive with those senses you have confined to yourself. I am here only to ask you to consider the possibility that your fear of the unknown or unseen is what is holding you back from opening fully to God and to your own divinity, as that living expression of Him.

Build your road, mankind. Allow yourself to trust that you will be cushioned by love on your journey. Allow yourself to seek more than you can conceive of now. Allow yourself to dream. Your dreams are magnificent, mankind. They are about your place in the grand scheme of things. Your dreams will help you to see what you can only hope for now. Build your road and then you will know.

In the heavens, at this moment of timing, there are wondrous things afoot. Mankind has entered into a pact with the light and has begun the journey homeward to the idea of God, in all the splendor and glory that before was only reserved for those gods placed on pedestals. You are now realizing that these gods that you worshiped were no different than you, save for one thing. They remembered who they were, and in so doing, could present themselves to you in all their glory because that is what they are...glorious. That is what you are, but you do not remember. There are many here at this time who are most anxious to wake you up! Will you allow this, mankind? Can you open yourself to the possibility that you are capable of being glorious and magnificent? Indeed, some of you are already identifying these terms and embracing them and becoming all that you are. There is a little known fact that is becoming known....finally becoming known. The dreamer is awakening from the dream. You are the dreamer, mankind, and the dream is what you now call your reality. The dream is that you are restricted to anything. The dream is that you cannot have all that you wish. The dream is that you are separate from the Father. Wake up! Please, wake up and become more than the dream.

So many lifetimes ago you were cautioned not to forget that you were part of the Father; that you were a creator on this plane of existence. When did you forget to create? When did you begin to doubt? When did you lose the ability to hear your Father speak to you...to call you? It is really so much water under the bridge now. Don't look back...look forward. But look forward with new eyes that vision only the light. You have called me forth, mankind. You have called many to come and to bear witness to your rebirth. The alignment of the energies that are brought forth, at this time, with your energies of renewal will catapult you into a new dimension of aware-ness. Is this not a wonderful time to be existing here? That you called us forth, are you not worthy and powerful? Own this knowledge and then you will know.

The stories that you will tell your children and grandchil-dren and great grandchildren are being written now with your awakening. Mankind, with this awareness comes the realiza-tion that your awakening has already happened. Time is a circle, a sphere that is existing simultaneously within the continuum. The continuum is, and ever shall be, ongoing. You are under the illusion, the dream, that you are in danger of failing this task. It is not so, for it has already been written. You are the authors....and you have written a most fascinating tale. I can hear your minds at work even now, trying to figure out how you can be the authors for an existence that is already established in the continuum of time, and coexisting with the past, the present and the future. It is not so difficult a concept when you begin to expand your understanding of what it is that makes the universes survive. If you share the belief that there is more in heaven and earth than you can now experience with your limited senses, then you will be open to the seed that I plant. Give up your need to understand for now. You cannot. You are not operating fully. It's as if you are a motor car with a very large engine and you are using bicycle pedals to operate it. You know it's supposed to move, you just don't know how it works and so you do the only thing that you understand...and you pedal.

It is alright for now. You are being shown how to start your engines, so to speak. Your job is to listen. Your job is to believe in yourself enough, and in your own divinity, so that you can be open for the information to come to you. That you now hold this book in your hand and are reading these pages, brings you closer to that understanding. Know this...if you want to continue to pedal your big motor car, that is alright too. If you wish, if you pray, if you believe that there is another way, then hold on and get ready to start your engines!

Mankind, there is so much light bombarding this planet now, that you would have to stand in a very deep hole not to be affected by it. Some of you are in a deep hole. Look up for just a second and take my hand. There is another way. Seek and you shall find. It is written...

A JOURNEY OF REMEMBRANCE

BE YE KNOWING

Be it known on this day that mankind has arisen to meet his Father. Be it known on this day that the Father has received His beloved children. He has gathered you up into His waiting arms. You are His once more, in full recognition of the fact that you were never separated from Him in the first place.

Be ye knowing of who you are, is your mantra from this day forward. Take comfort in the knowing and in the being. Live your life wisely and be in love with God once more, and be in love with the one who came to journey the journey called mankind. Be at peace with your reflection in the light. Take comfort from His love. I am Ezekiel and I welcome you home. So be it.

ABOUT THE AUTHOR

The author, J. L. Sibrian, lives quietly with her husband and son in Southern California. For the past 27 years she has worked in the field of education. Her spiritual studies began over ten years ago, and continue to this day. She has had many enlightened teachers who have helped her to grow and develop into the spititual seeker she is today. Through the publishing of this book, the author hopes to provide the opportunity for similar growth in others.